Would You Rather?

GROSS EDITION

Witty Jacob

Would you rather wear a farting school bag in school everyday

OR

have to confess infront of whole class that you pooped your pants?

Would you rather sneez everytime you talked to your crush

OR

cough for 5 minutes whenever you hug someone?

Would you rather eat snails for dinner every day

OR

sleep with snails all over you everynight?

Would you rather lick strangers hand

OR

lick the window of a bus?

Would you rather eat spiders

OR

shower with spiders?

Would you rather pet 10 snakes

OR

pet 10 cockroaches?

Would you rather drink pee that has bugs in

OR

drink 1 year old yougurt?

Would you rather have worms in a sandwich and eat them

OR

eat a hot dog made out of a pigeon meat?

Would you rather have
a bubble bath with
snakes inside

OR

with pirana inside?

Would you rather eat a booger from a friend

OR

a booger from your grandma?

Would you rather
eat a sandwich made
of fried bugs and mayo
with leeches

OR

a sandwich with 2
weeks old ham and
ketchup with nose hair?

Would you rather go to school with vomit in your school bag

OR

vomit in class in front of everybody while peeing in your pants?

Would you rather hold a slimy giant snail for 30 minutes

OR

hold dogs poop for 2 minutes?

Would you rather poke a beehive and stand in front of it for 30 minutest

OR

get locked in a dark room alone with rats for 2 hours?

Would you rather have a bath in pig pee

OR

have a bath in hot sauce?

Would you rather lick the hottest sauce on earth for 30 seconds

OR

lick rotten beef for 1 minute?

Would you rather smell sweaty footballers foot for an hour

OR

smell farts of babies for half an hour?

Would you rather eat cows tongue

OR

drink half of a bottle of hot sauce?

Would you rather eat worm spaghetti with a sauce made of rotten vegetables

OR

drink a gallon of soup made of bird's saliva.?

Would you rather have rotten food under your bed

OR

have a drawer full of bugs?

Would you rather
lick a pimple from
a stranger

OR

eat your friend's
earwax?

Would you rather have acne on your tongue

OR

have maggots all over your room?

Would you rather sprinkle grandad's dandruff on your pizza and eat it

OR

eat a pizza that smells and tastes like worst farts ever?

Would you rather pop a zit on your face in front of your crush

OR

pop your zit in a toilet where nobody sees you, and you eat it?

Would you rather find a hole in your bedroom wall full of smelly socks

OR

rotten food or find a hole with spiders in?

Would you rather eat sickening seafood and vomit for 2 days

OR

eat lice but you don't vomit?

Would you rather wear the same dirty clothes to school for a month

OR

have clean clothes but cannot shower for a month?

Would you rather have a scary clown hiding in your closet

OR

have a giant spider in your closet?

Would you rather eat beetles for dinner every day for a year

OR

eat rotten meat for dinner every day for 6 months?

Would you rather drink juice with bird saliva

OR

drink blood from ants?

Would you rather have killer ants in your hair

OR

have leeches in your hair?

eat beetles for dinner
every day for a year

OR

eat rotten meat for
dinner every day for
6 months?

Would you rather drink juice with bird saliva

OR

drink blood from ants?

Would you rather have killer ants in your hair

OR

have leeches in your hair?

Would you rather eat mac and cheese made with rotten smelly cheese

OR

eat a burger which patty is made out of cat meat?

Would you rather drink a smoothie made out of slugs and frogs blood

OR

a smoothie made out of rotten onions and lizards?

Would you rather wear a medical face mask from a homeless person

OR

a medical mask made out of old smelly socks?

Would you rather touch a 100-year-old mummy

OR

touch 50 years old zombie?

Would you rather go to school while farting every 2 minutes

OR

go to school while you have to poop every 20 minutes?

Would you rather have a slug for a pet

OR

have giant ants as a pet?

Would you rather eat ice cream made out of dog poo

OR

ice cream made out of ticks and saliva?

Would you rather drink orange juice with granddad's saliva in it in front of the whole school

OR

drink water with food scraps in?

Would you rather go to school with vomit all over you

OR

with a helmet made out of bird poop?

Would you rather sleep outside in the mud

OR

sleep inside in a bed full of snakes and maggots?

Would you rather go to a friend birthday party dressed in used toilet paper

OR

dressed in dead rats?

Would you rather pee on a bowling alley in front of the whole class

OR

poop in your friend's bag and nobody sees you?

Would you rather shower with water that has bed bugs

OR

shower with dog's pee?

Would you rather eat hair from your granddad

OR

hair from a mummy?

Would you rather sneeze every 30 seconds for 1 month

OR

cough every minute for 2 months?

Would you rather drink spider blood

OR

drink snake blood?

Would you rather watch your friend pop a giant zit and eat what comes out

OR

eat your own hair covered in friends boogers?

Would you rather have fall in a tank full of animal pee and poop

OR

fall in a tank full of rotten onions?

Would you rather swim in a pool full of slugs and bacteria

OR

full of rotten tomato juice and rats?

Would you rather clean an elephant space in the zoo

OR

clean a horse's space?

Would you rather
help to clean the school
toilet

OR

help to clean the school
kitchen?

Would you rather take a nap on dirty shoes from your school mates

OR

take a nap in a public toilet?

Would you rather drink water with mud

OR

leeches or eat mud with ants?

Would you rather clean tiger's poop

OR

clean giraffe's poop?

Would you rather go to a cinema and eat popcorn covered in slime

OR

go to a restaurant and eat steak with a sauce made of rats?

Would you rather make a cake out of mayo, grease, and dead bird

OR

with boogers, rotten tomatoes, and bad milk?

Would you ratherclean your brother's/sister's smelly feet

OR

massage homeless man feet for an hour?

Would you rather eat nuts with worms in it

OR

eat cherries with worms in it?

Would you rather smell baby poo for an hour

OR

smell your friend's feet and armpit for 2 hours?

Would you rather drink shake made out of chocolate that smells like poo and cat fur

OR

a shake made of bees and cows blood?

Would you rather
go to school smelling
like pee

OR

go to school smelling
like a dead animal?

Would you rather throw a rotten banana at your crush

OR

throw a dead rat at your friend?

Would you rather drink spoiled milk

OR

drink the super old fish sauce?

Would you rather be trapped in the belly of a giant

OR

be trapped in the belly of a whale?

Would you rather pick nose from your dad

OR

pick nose from your mom?

Would you rather have boogers with snails for dinner

OR

mash potatoes mixed with baby vomit and chicken liver?

Would you rather lick cat's fur and clean the cat

OR

lick horsetail for a 2 minutes?

Would you rather fart every time you see your crush

OR

burp every time you talk to your crush?

Would you rather wear used underwear for a month

OR

use someone else's toothbrush for 2 months?

Would you rather chew a gum that was made out of scabs

OR

a gum that was made out of maggots?

Would you rather burp in your favorite teacher's face

OR

fart in front of your crush?

Would you rather have pee coming out of your eyes

OR

poop coming out of your mouth ?

Would you rather fart in school 5 times a day really loudly

OR

smell farts of your grandma 10 times a day?

Would you rather eat soup made out of zombies

OR

a soup made out of spoiled milk and dead fish?

Would you rather eat what's under your nails

OR

eat bananas cover with boogers?

Would you rather have the face covered with fleas

OR

have the face covered in lice?

Would you rather scream whenever you talk

OR

lose the ability to lie?

Would you rather have
saliva in your juice

OR

have hamsters pee in
your juice?

Would you rather wear homeless person clothes for a week

OR

wear clothes dirty from pee and poop?

Would you rather have a fridge full of rotten food

OR

have a fridge full of dead flies?

Would you rather eat a burrito full of spiders

OR

a burrito with spoiled lizard meat?

Would you rather have corn flakes with spoiled milk

OR

have toast with smelly cheese in it?

Would you rather
eat bat's poop

OR

drink bat's pee?

Would you rather fart every morning for 30 minutes

OR

poop every night 5 times in a row?

Would you rather eat cheesecake made of cat poop

OR

pie made out of birds vomit?

Would you rather
drink glass of sweat
from your friend

OR

drink a glass of sweat
from your granddad?

Would you rather lick a dirty diper

OR

use a toothbrush from a school mate you dislike?

Would you rather bite off a friends zit

OR

never be able to eat sweets again?

Would you rather drink a glass of pee every morning and eat whatever you want

OR

only eat vegetables f or every meal?

Would you rather have bad smell in your room but its clean

OR

have dirty room but it smells good?

Would you rather eat crocodile skin

OR

drink crocodile pee ?

Would you rather suck on a frozen popsicle made out of rotten vegetable water

OR

suck on a popsicle that smells and taste like dirty socks ?

Would you rather shower once a year

OR

have 3 teeth missing for a year?

Would you rather eat bees and wasps at once

OR

eat soup made out of goat teeth and monkey brain?

Would you rather
sing in front of whole
school and make a fool
out of yourself

OR

wear dirty socks for a
year?

Would you rather start giving away free massages to homeless people

OR

eat 5 raw potatoes?

Printed in Great Britain
by Amazon

69684885R00059